I0527243

Frederick Octavius Prince

Bronze group commemorating emancipation

A gift to the city of Boston from Hon. Moses Kimball

Frederick Octavius Prince

Bronze group commemorating emancipation
A gift to the city of Boston from Hon. Moses Kimball

ISBN/EAN: 9783337141691

Printed in Europe, USA, Canada, Australia, Japan

Cover: Foto ©Andreas Hilbeck / pixelio.de

More available books at **www.hansebooks.com**

BRONZE GROUP

COMMEMORATING

EMANCIPATION

A GIFT TO THE CITY OF BOSTON

FROM

HON. MOSES KIMBALL.

Dedicated December 6, 1879.

PRINTED BY ORDER OF THE CITY COUNCIL.

1879.

ORATION,

BY HIS HONOR

FREDERICK O. PRINCE,

MAYOR.

———

Gentlemen of the City Council: —

FELLOW-CITIZENS, — We place to-day upon its pedestal this pleasing work of art, presented to the City of Boston by our fellow-citizen, the Honorable MOSES KIMBALL. The Municipal Council and the people are grateful to the munificent donor, and I have been requested to express their acknowledgments, and make such dedicatory remarks as seem appropriate to the occasion.

Mr. Kimball has attached a condition to his gift. He requires the city to make provision for its care and protection, and place it where the people "most do congregate," that they may be constantly reminded of the great event it commemorates; for it is his desire, by this memorial bronze, not only to adorn the city and gratify our sense of the beautiful, but to elevate and instruct the popular mind by its

solemn lessons of justice, philanthropy, and patriotism. Thus, in making the gift and directing its
location, his liberality and wisdom are equally conspicuous.

The city has agreed to comply with this condition.
The site selected is a thoroughfare, and meets the
approbation of the considerate donor. May this eloquent memorial endure as long as things made by
human hands are permitted to endure; as long as the
human mind retains its capacity to know that liberty
is the gift of Heaven to man, and that resistance to
tyranny is obedience to God.

The desire to record important events, and the
great actors therein, by some artistic expression, is
such a natural disposition, that all nations, civilized
and barbaric, have invoked architecture, sculpture,
painting, and poetry, to commemorate their eminent
sovereigns, soldiers, statesmen, philosophers, orators,
poets, and those who have rendered beneficial service
to the State and to humanity. Gratitude, pride, and
affection, are not satisfied to trust such commemo-
ration to a vehicle so uncertain as tradition. The
historic page informs only the student and the
lettered; but all can read and understand, with
more or less appreciation, the language of art. The
popular mind comprehends more readily an idea in
the concrete than the abstract, — an idea expressed

by sensuous forms than by words, however eloquent.
Art performs its highest office when it perpetuates
heroic action. National monuments are epic lessons
to future generations. They instruct, admonish, de-
light, and inspire. That which we dedicate to-day
speaks of the most important act in our annals, and
commemorates one of the great eras of the Republic,
— the *emancipation of four millions of slaves!*

It is fitting and appropriate that we should come
here to Faneuil Hall and have our dedicatory exer-
cises. The associations of this venerable and historic place accord with the solemn character of the
occasion. The walls which heard those denuncia-
tions of tyranny that led to the immortal declaration
— "All men are created free," — should echo our
thanksgiving that all men throughout our broad domain — of every race and color — are at last free,
and witness the consecration of the sculpture which
commemorates the event.

SLAVERY NOW INDEFENSIBLE.

The occasion does not require me to enter at
length into the causes which led to the great civil
war. I do not propose to discuss the right, moral or
legal, of one man to have property in another; nor
shall I have much to say upon the nature and influence of slavery, or the political or economic conse-

quences which have come from it. The opinions of
mankind upon the whole matter have been made up,
and are not to be changed. However much men
may differ as to forms of government, and the
administration of government, whatever divergence
of opinion may exist touching political measures and
political instrumentalities, no one in any part of the
world enlightened by Christian civilization will now
dare to defend slavery as a system of labor. It has
ceased to be ; but its death-struggles convulsed the
country as nothing else could, and provoked the
most dreadful of all wars, — civil war. Let it be
forgotten and buried with the dead past; and in its
grave let us put all the wild passions and bitter animosities it evoked. It was hostile to national union
and domestic peace ; but, now that its baleful influence is over, let us hope that we may be again one
people, politically and socially, so that we may be
the better able to work out our destiny and mission
among the nations of the earth. I propose to recall
to your attention at this time some of the causes
which led to emancipation.

When the Declaration of American Independence
was promulgated all the thirteen colonies were slave-
holding States. At the North it was generally believed that the proposition therein set forth, that all
men were born free, applied alike to the negro as

well as to the white man. In Massachusetts the
Supreme Court, reflecting the sentiments of the
Puritans and their steady devotion to the right of
personal liberty in all men, declared that not only the
slaves here were emancipated by that instrument,
but that they had been already made free, by the
adoption of the State Constitution and Bill of
Rights, previous to the formation of the Federal
Constitution.

In other Northern States similar judicial decisions
were made, and slavery soon ceased to exist therein.
It was otherwise at the South. The material prosperity of that portion of the country was thought to
depend upon the maintenance of slavery, for the time
at least; and, influenced by their supposed interests,
our southern brethren did not consider the declaration as universal in its operation, and therefore re-
stricted its application to white citizens alone.

Whoever inquires into the opinions and sentiments
of the leading minds of the country when the Federal Constitution was formed will find that slavery
was regarded everywhere as a political, if the enlightened sense of the people had not then begun to
consider it as a moral, evil. Thinking men, North
and South, believed its existence was a source of
national weakness, and that its influence on free
labor was unwholesome and depressing. Its ultimate

extinction was therefore desired and expected. Both
sections of the country deprecated the continuance
of the African slave-trade, from fear that the institution would be perpetuated to an indefinite period; for
the belief obtained that slavery would die out if the
slave-trade were abandoned.

OPINIONS OF THE EARLY SOUTHERN STATESMEN.

As early as 1772 the Legislature of Virginia had
memorialized the King of Great Britain upon the
dangers of slavery, and expressed the desire that the
slave-trade might be abolished; but the king replied,
"that, upon pain of his highest displeasure, the importation of slaves should not be in any respect ob-
structed." How are we to reconcile this declaration
from the crown with the decision of the English court
in 1772, in the celebrated Sommersett case, that no
man could make a slave of another? Well may
honest Ben Franklin indignantly say, "Pharisaical
Britain! to pride thyself in setting free a single slave
that happened to land on thy coast, while thy laws
continue a traffic whereby so many thousands are
dragged into a slavery that is entailed upon their
posterity."

As I have said, it was thought that slavery would
soon die out if the importation of slaves should
cease. When it was proposed in the Federal Con-

vention by some northern delegates that the slave-
trade should continue beyond the term of twenty
years, the southern members objected that the period
was too long. Mr. Madison was strongly of this
opinion, and so expressed himself. Jefferson said
during the war of the Revolution, "The way, I
hope, is preparing, under the auspices of Heaven, for
a total emancipation." At another time he confessed
that "he trembled for his country when he remembered
that God was just." Washington declared, "there
was not a man living who wished more sincerely than
he to see a plan adopted for the abolition of slavery."
Luther Martin and William Pinckney, the great law-
yers of Maryland, both advocated emancipation, —
the former in the Federal Convention of 1787, and
the latter in the Maryland House of Delegates in
1789. Mr. Iredell, of North Carolina, said in the
Constitutional Convention, " When the entire abolition of slavery takes place, it will be an event which
must be pleasing to every generous mind, and to
every friend of human nature." I might quote the
opinions of many other southern statesmen of that
day to the same effect. Mr. Webster observes in his
great speech on the Constitution and the Union,
" that the eminent men, the most eminent men, and
nearly all the conspicuous politicians of the South,
then held the same sentiments, — that slavery was an

evil, a blight, a scourge, and a curse. There are no
terms of reprobation of slavery so vehement in the
North at that day as in the South. The North was
not so excited against it as the South; and the reason is, I suppose, that there was much less of it at
the North, and the people did not see, or think they
saw, the evils so prominently as they were seen, or
thought to be seen, at the South."

Reverdy Johnson, Senator from Maryland, in his
memorable speech made on the 5th April, 1864, in the
Senate of the United States, on the constitutional
amendment abolishing slavery, said, "The men
who fought through the Revolution, those who
survived its perils and shared its glory, and who
were called to the convention by which the Constitution of the United States was drafted and rec-
ommended to the adoption of the American people,
almost without exception thought that slavery was
not only an evil to any people among whom it might
exist, but that it was an evil of the highest character,
which it was the duty of all Christian people, if possible, to remove, because it was a sin as well as an
evil. I think the history of those times will bear me
out in the statement, that if the men by whom the
Constitution was framed, and the people by whom it
was adopted, had anticipated the time in which we
live, they would have provided by constitutional enact-

ment that that evil and that sin should at some
comparatively unremote day be removed; . . .
they earnestly desired, not only upon grounds of
political economy, not only upon reasons material in
their character, but upon grounds of morality and
religion, that sooner or later the institution should
terminate." As further evidence of the state of public opinion contemporaneous with the formation of
the Constitution, I will add, that abolition societies
were then formed in most of the original thirteen
States; in Rhode Island, Connecticut, Maryland,
Virginia, Delaware, New York, and Pennsylvania.
That of the latter was formed as early as 1774, and
Dr. Franklin was its president. John Jay, Chief
Justice of the Supreme Court of the United States,
was the first, and Hamilton was the second, president
of the New York society.

But the most striking proof of the unanimity of
public sentiment throughout the country, South as
well as North, in regard to the ultimate extinction of
slavery, is to be found in the passage of the celebrated ordinance of 1787, by which slavery was forever excluded "from the whole territory over which
the Congress of the United States had jurisdiction."
And that was all the territory north-west of the
Ohio. *This ordinance was passed by the unanimous
concurrence of the whole South.* The vote of every

State in the Union was given in its favor, with the exception of a single individual vote, which was given by a *northern* man. "The ordinance," says Mr. Webster, "prohibiting slavery forever northwest of the Ohio has the hand and seal of every southern member of Congress."

PROVISIONS OF THE CONSTITUTION.

Notwithstanding these views of the southern people touching slavery as an institution, at the time the fathers were engaged in framing the Federal Constitution, they were not prepared for immediate emancipation. Objections were urged against it. It was thought that the economic interests of the South would suffer, for a time at least, by any such sweeping and radical change in their system of labor, and they were unwilling to risk the experiment. Guarantees for the protection of slavery were therefore demanded as the condition upon which they would adopt the political compact which was to "form a more perfect union," and make us one people.

There was much embarrassment in adjusting the matter so as to satisfy all parties. An agreement, however, was finally reached through mutual compromises, and the Constitution was ratified and adopted by all the States.

Three important propositions were thus established: —

First. — The recognition of slavery as it then
existed in the States, with full power in the States
over slavery within their respective limits.

Second. — The prohibition of slavery in all the territory then owned by the United States, through the
adoption of the ordinance of 1787.

Third. — The grant to the new government of
the power to abolish the slave-trade after a limited
period.

The ratification of the Constitution was concurrence on the part of both North and South in these
different propositions.

The new government being thus established, the
United States of America took a new departure, and
entered the family of nations as one sovereign power,
formed from many parts, and commenced a new
career of national life.

It had the blessings and prayers of all those in
every quarter of the globe who love liberty, and who
feel that civilization can only develop and advance
under its benign influence. The future seemed
surely " full of joy and promise and sunshine." The
genius of the people, their ardent love of liberty,
their hardy virtues, their indomitable courage, ever
reliable for the defence of their political rights, their

form of government so admirably adapted for the
development of all that makes a nation powerful and
prosperous, their varied climate, their vast resources,
their fortunate geographical position, with the wide
Atlantic between them and the old feudal world, and
the national polity inspired by the genius of Washington, which avoided all entangling alliances, — all
promised centuries of happy, prosperous, and glorious
national life.   The Saturnian age was to return
again.

But there were those whose judgments were not
wholly controlled by these high hopes and pleasing
anticipations. They saw, from the beginning, beneath
the surface of this halcyon sea, and not far below it,
hidden and dangerous rocks that lay in the path of
the ship of state.   They felt that the government,
with all its apparent exemption from the causes of
national decline and decay, with all its seeming pos-
session of assured and immortal life, was, like the
divinely born Grecian hero, vulnerable in one place
at least, — in that feature of its organization which
compelled the recognition and protection of slavery.
They could not see how such potent antagonisms as
Slavery and Freedom could long continue to exist side
by side; and they felt that, sooner or later, either the
encroaching freedom of the North must dominate
the South, or the encroaching slavery of the South

must dominate the North, despite of covenants, compromises, compacts, and constitutions.

THE IRREPRESSIBLE CONFLICT.

The event corresponded with their predictions. "No great political or moral revolution," says a distinguished essayist, "has ever occurred, which has not been accompanied by its prognostic." Such soon appeared, foreshowing the great change which was to come over the southern mind with respect, not only to the policy of maintaining slavery as a system of labor, but to the moral right to do so. Cotton, which was not considered a commercial product of the South at the adoption of the Constitution, was found, after the invention of the cotton gin, so adapted to the climate of the slave States as practically to give them a monopoly of its cultivation. It was soon discovered that here was an inexhaustible mine of wealth. All that was needed for its development was cheap labor, and it was believed that such could be only found in slave labor. The entire policy of the South in respect to the institution immediately changed, and all their thoughts and efforts were directed to its protection and extension. For this purpose new territories were acquired and new States admitted into the Union. The political power of the South was thus greatly augmented, and

the North, alarmed lest slavery should be national-
ized, organized to prevent its further extension.

These two opposing forces soon generated an
"irrepressible conflict."

Both sides complained of each other.   Each
charged broken faith and violations of the constitutional compact.   When time shall soften the prejudices and calm the passions engendered in the
unnatural strife, so that the conduct of both parties
can be examined with judicial impartiality, the his-
torian will be able to set forth all the facts and make
up the record.   We are too near the events; we
share too largely, both at the North and the South,
the feelings and opinions which inaugurated the
strife, to enable us to make proper discrimination.
The verdict must be rendered by another generation;
but there is one fact about which there can be no
dispute.   The South, alleging that slavery and their
interests were endangered by the election of Mr.
Lincoln to the Presidency, and the access to power
of the Republican party, and claiming the right of
secession, made war upon the flag.   Thereupon, the
administration, in obedience to the mandates of the
Constitution, marshalled its forces for the maintenance of the Federal authority and the preservation
of the Union.   Civil war was thus inaugurated.

Among the questions involved in this terrible controversy, which the student of history may perhaps raise, will be, whether this conflict could have been avoided by any different statesmanship, notwithstanding the intense feeling respecting slavery which divided the people of the two sections, and the hostile spirit which animated them.

It may be asked, if slavery be regarded as the predisponent, as well as the immediate cause of the war, whether it would not ere long have died out under the advancing civilization of the age, which was fast destroying the conditions under which it could alone exist? Would not the progress of moral ideas, and the enlightened opinions of mankind, have made it impossible for any nation, especially the English-speaking race, to uphold forever the hideous institution?

Data might perhaps be found for such speculation in the changed sentiments of the northern tier of slave States during the decade preceding the war, touching the right to hold property in man, and the policy of maintaining this system of labor, and in the significant fact that the slaves were fast disappearing from this section of the country. The recent action of Russia, Spain, Brazil, and other nations, might be cited to show the great changes in public opinion in respect to the institution. In Cuba all slaves over sixty years of age have been manumitted; and within a few days the Spanish Minister of Colonies presented to the Senate at Madrid the government bill, touching the abolition of slavery in Cuba, remarking that "it was contrary to the laws of nature, and could no longer be maintained in the civilized world." Surely, the world moves! Perhaps it will be found, upon careful examination of all the facts, that slavery was rather the exciting than the actual cause of the strife between the North and the South, and that deeper down there were the same forces at work for the accomplishment of this result, which threatened nullification and secession in 1830, and which would have then led to civil war but for the eloquence of Webster, and the firmness of Jackson.

LINCOLN NOT AN EXTREMIST.

Mr. Lincoln, when elected President of the United States, was not an abolitionist in the extreme sense of the term. He was not of the *higher-law* party. He was opposed to slavery — morally and politically. He believed the Declaration of Independence operated equally upon all men, without regard to color; and while he was opposed to the extension of slavery into new States and territories, he recognized fully the binding force of the compromises under which the Constitution was adopted, and the protection

which that compact gave slavery in the States where
it existed. He had no disposition or intention to
molest or interfere in any way with the institution
there. He repeatedly defined his position on this
question in his speeches in the political campaigns
previous to his election, and so clearly and unam-
biguously that he could not be misunderstood.

In the celebrated debate with Mr. Douglas, when
they were both candidates for the United States
Senate, Judge Douglas asked him whether he then
stood, as he stood in 1854, in favor of the unconditional repeal of the fugitive slave law; and he replied, " I do not now nor ever did stand in favor of
the unconditional repeal of the fugitive slave law."
Judge Douglas then asked him if he stood pledged,
as in 1854, against the admission of any more slave
States into the Union; and he answered, " I do not
now nor ever did stand pledged against the admission of any more slave States." He further said that
he was not pledged to the abolition of slavery in the
District of Columbia, nor to the prohibition of the
slave-trade between the States.

These declarations were not satisfactory to the
radical anti-slavery men; for they showed most con-
clusively that he did not belong to that political
church.

In his address at Cincinnati, in 1859, he said, " I

am not what they call, as I understand it, a black
Republican, but I think slavery wrong, morally and
politically;" and, referring to some Kentuckians present, observed, "We Republicans mean to treat you,
as near as we possibly can, as Washington, Jefferson,
and Madison, treated you. We mean to leave you
alone, and in no way interfere with your institution;
to abide by all and every compromise of the Constitution."

In his remarks to the Mayor and Common Council
of Washington, just after his election as President,
he assured them that the people should have all
their rights; "not grudgingly, but fully and fairly."

In his first inaugural, and in his proclamation, he
says, "Apprehension seems to exist among the
people of the Southern States, that by the accession
of a Republican administration their property and
their peace and personal security are to be endangered. There never has been any reasonable
cause for such apprehension. Indeed, the most
ample evidence to the contrary has all the while
existed, and been open to their inspection. It is
found in nearly all the published speeches of him
who now addresses you. I do but quote from one
of those speeches when I declare, that 'I have no
purpose, directly or indirectly, to interfere with the
institution of slavery in the States where it now

exists.' I believe I have no lawful right to do so, and I have no inclination to do so. Those who nominated and elected me did so with the full knowledge that I had made this and similar declarations, and had never recanted them; and, more than this, they placed in the platform for my acceptance, and as a law to themselves and to me, the clear and emphatic resolution which I now read: —

" ' *Resolved*, That the 'maintenance inviolate of the rights of the States, and especially of the rights of each State, to order and control its own domestic institutions according to its own judgment exclusively, is essential to that balance of power on which the perfection and endurance of our political fabric depends; and we denounce the lawless invasion by armed force of the soil of any State or territory, no matter under what pretext, as among the gravest crimes.'

" I now reiterate these sentiments, and in doing so I only press upon the public attention the most conclusive evidence of which the case is susceptible, that the property, peace, and security, of no section are to be in anywise endangered by the now incoming administration."

THE POSITION OF THE REPUBLICAN PARTY.

Whatever the South may have feared from the

extreme men around Mr. Lincoln, they had, or could have had, no apprehension that he would not stand squarely and firmly by his opinions and promises on this great question; for if there was any trait of character, any one virtue, for which he was especially noted, it was his honesty and fidelity to truth. These qualities were conspicuous through all his checkered and unblemished life, from the time when, poor and struggling for existence, he followed the hard fortunes of the flat-boatman on the Mississippi; through all his honorable career as a lawyer and a legislator, until elected to the highest office in the gift of the people. When he took the oath upon his inauguration to " preserve, protect, and defend, the Constitution of the United States," he took it, as he says, " with no mental reservations, and with no purpose to construe the Constitution or laws by any hypercritical rules." Can any one doubt that he intended from the beginning to keep this solemn oath, and to administer the government honestly, fairly, and according to the requirements of the Constitution?

It is thus evident that there was no design on the part of the Republican party to interfere, upon their accession to power, with slavery in the States where it then existed. Furthermore, if they had such design they could not have executed it. Gov. Perry,

of South Carolina, well said, "The rights of the
South were in no possible danger, even had Mr.
Lincoln been disposed to interfere with them. There
was at that time a majority of twenty-seven in the
House of Representatives politically opposed to him.
There was a majority in the Senate of six opposed
to him. A majority of the Supreme Court were
opposed to the principles of the Republican party.
A large majority of the people had supported others
for the Presidency. He was powerless to injure the
slave States." Some of the more radical members of
the party might have proposed, in their hostility to
the institution, violent and unconstitutional measures;
but they were inconsiderable in numbers and without controlling influence.

It was the duty of the government to defend itself
against all assaults of its enemies, foreign and
domestic,— to maintain the Union of the States,—
and it was bound to use all powers and means within
its control necessary for the purpose. When, therefore, the war came, the executive summoned the military force of the country for its protection ; but it
was not until the contest had continued for nearly
two years; until a vast amount of treasure and blood
had been expended, and it had been proved that the
armies of the republic were inadequate for the sup-
pression of this gigantic revolt, that the President,

as a last resource, adopted the expedient of emancipation.

All his conduct shows that, in taking this important step, Mr. Lincoln did not move hastily, like a partisan, who was impatiently seeking for the opportunity to abolish slavery; but slowly, cautiously, and reluctantly, as a statesman should, who appreciated the solemn magnitude of the measure, and saw the momentous consequences which would follow it. He reflected long and seriously before acting. He conscientiously considered the obligations of his official oath and the demands of duty.

THE POSTPONEMENT OF EMANCIPATION.

No political, party, or other improper considerations were permitted to influence his judgment or control his action. So careful was he not to err in the matter, it was thought by many, not extreme in their views, that the cause of the Union suffered by his delay. But in so grave an exigency he preferred to err on what he deemed the safest side. When therefore General Fremont issued his order, in August, 1861, declaring the slaves of the Missouri insurgents to be thereafter free, Lincoln, regarding the measure premature and impolitic, although he believed it was competent to adopt it under the war powers of the Constitution, did not then think it an "indispensable necessity," and directed its modification.

When, a little later, General Cameron, the Secretary of War, suggested the arming of the negroes, he did not think this an "indispensable necessity," and objected to the proposal.

When, still later, General Hunter made his proclamation and order declaring all the slaves in South Carolina, Georgia, and Florida free forever, he annulled it, "not thinking the indispensable necessity had come." On the question of emancipating and arming negroes, he said, "The Union must be preserved, and all indispensable means must be used; but I deprecate haste in the use of extreme measures, which might reach the loyal as well as the disloyal."

It will be remembered that the public sentiment was becoming daily more and more intense in the demand for immediate and unconditional emancipation as the shortest and surest way of bringing the war to an end. It was urged that the crushing of slavery would be the crushing of the rebellion. It was claimed that emancipation would bring into the Union ranks hundreds of thousands of colored men. The more violent of the Republican newspapers denounced Mr. Lincoln for remissness and inaction. He replied in his defence, "My paramount object is to save the Union, and not either to save or destroy slavery. If I could save the Union, without freeing any slave, I would do it; if I could save it by freeing all the slaves I would do it; and if I could save it by freeing some, and leaving others alone, I would do it."

Notwithstanding all the pressure upon him for the issue of the Proclamation of Emancipation, he still hastens slowly. He waits until he could put the slave party clearly in the wrong; until the South had passed the Rubicon; until it was evident that the insurgents would never abandon the contest; until the war had been so waged as to leave no alternative but to yield the cause, and allow the Union to be broken up and destroyed.

I recall all this to your attention to show how carefully and cautiously he reached his determination to adopt the measure of emancipation. When he finally resolved upon it he gave ample notice of his intention, that those who would be affected by its operation might save themselves, if they wished to do so. After months went by, with no signs of surrender, and no indication that the enemies of the Union and the republic would return to their allegiance, declaring that "he sincerely believed it to be an act of justice, warranted by the Constitution upon military necessity, upon which he invoked the considerate judgment of mankind and the gracious favor of Almighty God," he issued the Proclamation of Emancipation.

The bolt was launched which was certain to end the war, destroy secession, vindicate the national authority, and save the Union.

EMANCIPATION A WAR MEASURE.

It is not necessary to consider the right of government to resort to emancipation as a war measure. I will only briefly say, that it is not to be denied that, under the circumstances, it was fitting and proper; that it was, as Mr. Lincoln said, justified as a military necessity. It was approved by Congress by a resolution passed by a large majority, and the country has endorsed it.

War existed between the United States and the seceding States; and the Supreme Court of the United States held, in 1863, in the case of the Hiawatha, "that where the course of justice is interrupted by revolt, rebellion, or insurrection, so that the courts of justice cannot be kept open, civil war exists, and hostilities may be prosecuted on the same footing as if those opposing the government were foreign enemies. All persons residing in the insurgent States are liable to be treated as enemies. . . . They are none the less enemies because they are traitors."

By the laws of war, the property of both enemies

and friends may be taken when needed. If slaves
were property, then the government could by these
laws take them to help subdue the enemy; their lib-
eration would obviously weaken the latter and
strengthen the former. The Constitution gives the
Executive belligerent powers *flagrante bello*, and he
is the sole judge whether the exigency exists for the
exercise of these powers. The only limit to the war
powers is to be found in the law of nations; and by
the law of nations, and the practice of belligerents
in modern times, the slaves of an enemy may be liberated in time of war by military power. This
power was exercised by England in the revolution-
ary war, and in the State of Virginia alone more .
than thirty thousand slaves were thus liberated.
Jefferson himself conceded that England had this
right. England again exercised this right in the
war of 1812. France did the same in her wars with
England, and some of the South American republics
have also exercised this right, and it has been recognized and admitted by all publicists. I do not understand that it is denied at the South.

It may be asked, whether it was *expedient* and
politic to issue the proclamation. If we recur to
the condition of things at the time, the question will
be readily answered. The government had been
trying for nearly two years to subdue the rebellion.

Immense sums of money had been expended. Many hundred thousand soldiers had been called out. Many fierce and sanguinary battles had been fought. The war had assumed gigantic proportions, and extended over a vast area of territory. Eleven States were in revolt. All their resources of men and money were levied. The "cradle and the grave" had been robbed for recruits. The most inflexible determination had been everywhere shown to surrender only when conquered. Foreign intervention was threatened. It may be doubted whether the Union could be saved by the means within the control of the government unless the enemy were deprived of the aid of the slaves, — for the latter were a great source of power; they raised the supplies for carrying on hostilities; they constructed military works, and served in the armies. Emancipation would transfer these allies to the national flag, and strengthen the national ranks by vast numbers of willing recruits. There can be no doubt, then, that it was our *policy*, as it was our right, to proclaim freedom to the negroes.

EFFECT OF THE PROCLAMATION.

Once free they could not be again enslaved, for the right of the slave to his freedom after being liberated is not to be disputed; and, furthermore, it would

be most atrocious as well as unjust, that he who had
once worn the uniform of a United States soldier,
and carried the flag through the carnage of battle,
should be again enslaved upon the recurrence of the
peace which he had helped to conquer. It may be
here observed that the Confederate Congress, in the
last hours of the war, passed a bill authorizing the
employment of slaves as soldiers, although the measure was adopted too late to help their cause. But in
the debate upon the bill it was conceded that " to
arm the negroes is to give them freedom. When
they come out scarred from the conflict they must be
free."

Furthermore, it is not to be denied that the government is at all times entitled to the aid of all those
it protects in its hour of danger. The black man is
as much bound as the white man to perform military
duty. There is no discrimination. When the common safety is imperilled, all alike must respond to
the call of patriotism.

The sequel demonstrated the wisdom of emancipation. As soon as the proclamation was issued, the
power of the rebellion was broken. The capacity
of the insurgents to continue the contest weakened,
and was soon destroyed. Both parties soon saw that
further resistance to the national arms could not
long be maintained. Emancipation, by thus short-

ening the war, saved thousands of lives, and a vast increase of national debt.

RIGHT OF SECESSION.

It should be remembered that the Southerners always denied that they were revolutionists. They justified, or attempted to justify, their action in taking arms against the government, by the right of secession, which, through their interpretation of the Federal Constitution, belonged to all the States.

It was claimed that, after the passage of the secession ordinances by the slave States, the latter resumed all the sovereignty which they possessed before the adoption of the Constitution, and that when they united and established the Southern Confederacy, it became *de jure* — as it was during the years of the war *de facto* — an independent autonomy; that upon this theory the contest was not a rebellion, but a war between two nationalities. Beyond question a large part of the southern people honestly believed in this alleged right of secession. Their political leaders, of the school of Haynes and Calhoun, had long maintained the construction of the Constitution which gave this right, and the public mind in that section of the country had become so thoroughly imbued and saturated with this heresy

that the people were united and fixed in their determination to maintain this right.

We of the North, under the teachings of our
statesmen, denied that a State, for any cause, could
secede. We are especially indebted to Daniel Webster for our political instruction and guidance here.
Previous to his masterly exposition of the nature
and genius of the Federal Constitution, the character
of that instrument, and its effects upon the States,
and the relation of the States to each other and to
the central government, and the respective rights and
obligations of each, were imperfectly understood.
He demonstrated that this political compact established something more than a confederation. He
proved, to the people of the North at least, that it
created a national unity, and established a national
government, notwithstanding it reserved to the States
certain powers and remains of sovereignty for the
control of their local and domestic affairs; and that
the union thus created could not be dissolved except
by the consent of all the States or by revolution.

This exposition was generally accepted by the
country north of the slave line, and fostered, if it did
not create, that patriotic and national sentiment to
which appeal was so successfully made when the flag
was assailed and the war inaugurated. The whole
North being a unit against secession, all its patri-

otism was aroused, and all its vast resources of men,
money, and military material contributed to the cause
without stint. Every draft upon its loyalty for the
defence of the government and the maintenance of
the Union was recognized.

It may be doubted whether there would have been
this unanimity of sentiment in respect to the rights
of the general government, or the same inflexible determination to maintain them, if the war of secession
had come upon our country at an earlier period of
our history, and before the theory of *nationality* had
fully formed and crystallized.

When we consider how fixed the two sections
were in their convictions touching their constitutional
rights, and remember the intensity of the popular
feeling therein; the fierce invective of the.press; the
acrimony of Congressional debate, and all the circumstances which surrounded and controlled the
question, — it is evident that its peaceful solution
could hardly be expected; that compromise was
almost impossible; that the Gordian knot could not
be untied, and was to be cut by the sword.

THE DECISION OF THE WAR.

The war has decided that there shall be no question or differences of opinion as to the loyalty due
from the States and from the people to the national

government. It has decided that there is no right
of secession. It has decided that slavery, which
prompted the assertion of this right, shall cease to
exist.

These decisions will never be disturbed. They are
final and irreversible. The dogma of secession was
the logical sequence of the doctrine of strict construction. The advocates of the latter maintained
the absurd proposition, that the framers of a constitution for the formation " of a more perfect union "
contrived such a monstrosity as a government without the powers necessary for its existence; that they
called into being an entity incapable of maintaining
itself against the revolt of its own parts, — a creation
which might be destroyed, like the children of Sat-
urn, as soon as born; a something that might at once
become a nothing.

If this be so, then all the time and labor of the
constitutional convention were expended in vain, for
its boasted work is of little value. What folly to
adopt a national flag, and demand for the United
States a place among the sovereignties of the world,
if any State, or any number of States, could at
pleasure break up the government and destroy its
unity and individuality!

But the framers of the Constitution were wise men,
and understood government as a science. By this

instrument they gave the federation all powers of a national character for the enforcement of national authority, and thus provided for the preservation of the Union. "Perpetuity," says Mr. Lincoln, "is implied, if not expressed, in the fundamental law of all national governments."

But while the rights of the national government have been adjusted, and the powers which properly belong to it recognized, through the arbitrament of war, a grave question looms in the distance, whether, in the flush of victory, it is not disposed to claim more than belongs to it; whether it may not encroach upon those rights which under the Constitution are reserved to the States. The preponderance of the centripetal may work as much of mischief in our political system as that of the centrifugal forces.

Soon after the adoption of the Constitution it was provided by amendment, "that the powers not delegated to the United States by the Constitution, nor prohibited by it to the States, are reserved to the States respectively or to the people." Our political system, as the Supreme Court of the United States has well said, "is an indestructible union composed of indestructible States." In the distribution of national and State powers we should watch with equal vigilance, that the rights and powers of the federal government are not disturbed by the States,

and that the rights and powers of the States are not
disturbed by the government. A just equilibrium
between both is essential for the protection of both.
Power ever seeks to augment itself. The path of
history is strewn with the wreck of governments
once free, which have been destroyed by executive
usurpation. To establish the just authority of the
national government we have expended thousands of
millions of treasure and fought hundreds of battles.
Let us take care that in avoiding one extreme we
do not drift into another, which may require like
sacrifices to correct. Our national safety lies in the
middle path. If the general government is permitted to usurp the reserved rights of the States
in matters of local and domestic concern, where the
latter have exclusive cognizance, each act of usurpation will become the precedent for another. Encroachment will follow encroachment, until the
harmony of the system is destroyed, and the government perverted from a union of coördinate and
coequal parts, each recognizing its loyal obligations
to the Union, and the Union in turn protecting the
rights of each, into a centralized and consolidated
authority, which will ultimately assert imperial sway,
to the destruction of constitutional government, and
the overthrow of free institutions. An "indestructible union of indestructible States" will give peace,

prosperity, and glory. The States, free and independent in their own spheres, and in the enjoyment of their just rights, will revolve in their appropriate orbits around the common centre of the national government, whose attracting and repelling forces, so adjusted as to maintain their proper influences over each portion of the system, will keep the whole in subordinate and harmonious relations.

EMANCIPATION MARKS A NATIONAL ERA.

The abolition of slavery may be said to make one of our national eras. The establishment of American Independence relieved us from the dwarfing influence of colonial dependence and the oppressions of imperial power. The emancipation of four millions of slaves delivered us from a dangerous disease, which threatened the national life. None will deny the baleful influence of slavery. It was an incubus upon the prosperity of the country. It retarded the development of its resources. It depressed values. It degraded labor, and affected injuriously every economic interest. There can be no doubt that the industries of the South were largely stimulated by this system of labor; but I think it can be shown that such prosperity as the slave States enjoyed was not attained by, but in spite of, slavery.

RESULT OF EMANCIPATION.

Now that this cause of evil has been removed we may hope that no great impediment to our advance in all the things which make a nation great and prosperous will be found. There may be sectional rivalries and differences of opinion touching many matters of national concern. The people of different States may not agree as to the policy which should govern in respect to fiscal measures, tariffs, the disposition of public lands, the construction of public works, the acquisition of new territory, the maintenance of armies and navies, and other questions of national polity; but these will be powerless to endanger the national existence; they will not be rocks and shoals to endanger the course of the ship of state, but merely storms through which statesmanship will safely guide and carry it. We may now hope, if we act wisely, for the perpetuity of the Union for as many centuries as the institutions of human contrivance can be expected to endure. The territory we occupy has been so shaped by Providence, its configuration is so peculiar, its mountain ranges and river valleys so formed, as to afford no national boundaries, and compel the Union as a necessity. We cannot divide into separate sovereignties. This natural adhesion is strengthened by the bond to be found in the influence of the Puritan spirit which pervades the country. Two-thirds of our people trace their lineage to the race which landed from the Mayflower. From the lakes to the gulf, and between the two oceans, the public mind and heart are imbued with the great qualities of these heroic men, — their love of liberty, their respect for law, their capacity for labor, their dauntless courage, their self-reliance, and their individuality.

Puritanism absorbs and proselytes. Its characteristics have been forced upon the fifty millions who now occupy our continental domain. We may therefore anticipate a brilliant future. The recuperative powers of the country are everywhere active. The wounds of war are healing. Our vast resources are developing. A million of soldiers have returned to the ranks of civil life, and become producers. The manufacturer, the farmer, the mechanic, all the workers in the various fields of labor, are promoting the national industries. The vast debt incurred in defence of the Union has been largely lessened. Our enormous exports are bringing daily and hourly to our shores the wealth of transatlantic countries. We have only to be true to ourselves, act justly, and cultivate peace, to become the leading nation of the world in all that makes a nation great and prosperous.

But, while we indulge these pleasing anticipations
and picture to ourselves the brilliant promises of the
political future, let us not forget the claims of the
four millions of slaves liberated by the emancipation,
symbolized by the bronze we dedicate to-day: Let
us not forget that they are now endowed with the
same " inalienable rights of life, liberty, and the pur-
suit of happiness," the same right to enjoy in " safety
and tranquillity the blessings of life," which the
white man enjoys. Under the amendments of the
Constitution they are American citizens, subject to
the obligations of citizenship and entitled to its
privileges.

Since their manumission they have shown themselves generally disposed to be orderly and well
behaved. Their peculiar physical organization requires them to live in the southern climate. They
must be, for the most part, agriculturists. Their
labor is necessary for the prosperity of the South.
Without it the rich lands of that section will depre-
ciate in value, for the white laborers cannot well fill
their places. That they are industrious is proved by
the fact that the largest crop of southern staples
ever raised was gathered the present year. Policy,
then, as well as justice, demands the good treatment
of the freedmen, the recognition of their rights, and
the protection of their interests.

But it is not merely their material welfare which should concern the people of this country. In order to make them good citizens and fit them for the discharge of the duties of citizenship, and especially to fit them for the judicious exercise of the right of suffrage, which has been recently extended to them through the amendments of the Constitution, they should be educated. Not only their own interests demand this, but the national safety calls for it as a necessity.

It is universally admitted that the moral and intellectual education of the people can alone uphold republican institutions. Whatever, then, is done for the elevation of the white should also be done for that of the colored men. They have been called the " wards of the nation." Let the nation treat them with a guardian's care, and see to it that they are trained and educated like other human beings, and taught to be honest, truthful, virtuous, and God-fearing.

The South, because of the poverty resulting from war, cannot, at this time, do all that is necessary in this direction; but the reports of the trustees of the Peabody Education Fund show that it realizes its obligations in the premises, and has made commendable progress in the work.

It is to be hoped that the general government will

soon see that it is its duty, as well as its interest, to aid our southern brethren in their efforts to discharge the solemn responsibilities imposed upon them by emancipation.

PERSONAL CHARACTER OF LINCOLN.

Allow me a few words touching the personal character of Mr. Lincoln. Those who have acted important parts in the drama of public affairs can rarely be justly understood or appreciated by their contemporaries. The latter are too near the scene of events to see them in their just proportions and relations; too greatly affected by the passions engendered in the conflict of opinions to perceive the facts as they exist; too often misled by the prejudices of party spirit to judge motives and measures with the candor which truth demands, and too strongly wedded to favorite theories and preconceived judgments to feel the full force of reason. Great statesmen especially, who have been in advance of their times, and devised governmental politics and systems whose fruition is in the future, have been compelled to look to posterity for appreciation, and, like Bacon, to leave "their names and memories to men's charitable speeches, and to foreign nations and the next age." Hence we find that the opinions touching the public men of preceding generations are often greatly modified

when history has gathered all the facts and data—
winnowed the true from the false, and made up its
record.

There have been, however, exceptional cases
where great qualities and splendid achievements
have been so conspicuous as to receive at once full
popular recognition. Our earlier annals are distinguished by a few of them. Washington and Franklin and Hamilton were all appreciated in their day
and generation. We of to-day can add to the illustrious constellation the revered name of Lincoln.
His individuality was so marked, his moral and intellectual character so fully recognized, and his
motives and conduct so well understood, that all
knew and saw him as he was,—a man of strong natural powers of mind, of fixed principles, of great
purity of character, and of dauntless moral courage,
who hated every species of injustice and wrong. No
time is wanted to understand him. No time is required to obliterate blots which impair his fame.
There is little in his public conduct to be excused or
forgotten. His place in the Pantheon of illustrious
benefactors is by general consent assured.

Such is the judgment of to-day, and such will
be the judgment of posterity and future ages. Those
of the North who were politically opposed to him, and
who, under the prejudices and passions of the hour,

misunderstood his motives, assailed his statesmanship, and condemned his management of the great questions he was called to solve, now largely admit he was misjudged, and concede to him the credit to which he is entitled. Even our brethren of the South, notwithstanding the animosities of war, are disposed to recognize his claim to the respect, admiration, and gratitude of the country.

In looking through his character we find most conspicuous his pure and lofty patriotism. He loved his country with all his heart and soul and mind. We can believe him when he said, standing in the hall whence the Declaration of Independence was issued, "I never had a feeling, politically, that did not spring from the sentiments embodied in that instrument. If the country cannot be saved upon its principles, I would rather be assassinated on the spot." All he said and did, both before and after he reached the Presidency, showed that he kept the political truths and the political principles embodied in the sublime Declaration constantly before him as his inspiration and guide. He was, without doubt, ambitious; but his ambition was of a generous and lofty character, ever subordinated to the single desire to serve his country and advance its best interests. He did not seek to raise himself to power by subverting the laws and trampling on the rights of the people, like so

many recorded by history in her most mournful pages;
nor did he resemble him so graphically described by
Lucan as rejoicing to have made his way by ruin, —

" Gaudet viam fecisse ruinâ."

He looked for advancement from the gratitude of the
nation, and sought the fame of the patriot who is
solicitous for the common good, and devoted to the
interests of the State. He wished not to destroy, but
to preserve.

HIS INTELLECTUAL QUALITIES.

Mr. Lincoln's early life was a hard struggle against
poverty. He had none of the advantages of early
education, and few opportunities for mental culture
until long after he reached manhood, for all his
time and energies were occupied in getting a liveli-
hood. He never acquired any great amount of learning. In respect to many subjects he may be said to
have been very ignorant; but such was the force of
his natural capacity, and the clear and logical character of his mind, that he may be placed in the ranks
of those described by Tully, " who, without learning,
by the almost divine instinct of their own mere nature,
have been of their own accord, as it were, judicious
and wise men; for nature, without learning, often

does more to lead men to credit and virtue, than learning when not assisted by a good natural capacity."

He read but few books, but it is evident that he
digested well what he read. He mastered principles,
and applied them to the subject under consideration
with exquisite accuracy. What he knew he knew
well and thoroughly. It could not be said that he
was learned in his profession, but he acquired the
reputation of being a sound and safe lawyer. As a
nisi prius lawyer he was very eminent, and few of
those who practised at the same bar with him had
greater power or more success with juries, whether
he attempted to convince or persuade.

A large share of his attention was given to the
study of politics and questions of government. His
public speeches and writings showed he had thought
long and deeply on these subjects, and comprehended
them so well that he was equally fitted for legislation
and administration. He was the Palinurus of the
ship of state, and through his good judgment, discre-
tion, and firmness, it was able to weather the dangers
which threatened its destruction. Like the Trojan
pilot, also, he was heedless of his own safety in the
discharge of his duty, and in the care of the trust
committed to his charge; and, alas! like him, too, he
was destined to sacrifice his life to the cause of his
country.

HIS MORAL QUALITIES.

His moral seems to have been more fully developed than his intellectual nature. All the accounts represent him as "kindly affectioned," tender-hearted, full of sweet and gentle charities, ever ready to sympathize with the heavy-laden and afflicted. His early struggles in life made him appreciate the sufferings of the poor, and he felt for them.

He was a plain, rough man, simple in his habits and ways, of incorruptible integrity, with a strong sense of justice and a conscientious regard for truth. It has been said, by those who knew him well, that he appreciated so fully the beauty of the right, and the deformity of the wrong, that, able and eloquent as he was as an advocate, he could not argue a case to the jury with his usual force when he felt he was on the wrong side. He could not be strong in the championship of a bad cause. He could not, like Belial,

> " Make the worse appear
> The better reason."

"On the right side of a case," said a competent critic, " he is an overwhelming giant; on the wrong side, his sense of justice and right makes him weak."

So well known was his character in these respects, that the people in his section of the country all knew

him and spoke of him as "Honest Old Abe." He
never corrupted his intellectual or moral nature,
either by doing wrong that good might come from
it, or by advocating error because it was popular;
and his statesmanship, always practical and straight-
forward, showed how unswervingly he followed what
was just and right.

There seems to have been no *vindictiveness* in his
nature. He was ever for mercy. His tenderness to
those who had endangered the safety of our armies,
by desertion and other military crimes, was almost
culpable. And it is owing to his forgiving nature
that there was no prosecution and punishment of
those who had made war upon the government.
When it was urged that the Nemesis demanded Jefferson Davis should atone for the terrible sufferings
he had brought upon the country, he replied, in the
sublimest strain of Christian charity, "Judge not,
lest ye be judged." On one occasion a friend was
denouncing his enemies. Lincoln said to him, "Hold
on; remember what St. Paul says: 'And now abideth
faith, hope, and charity. But the greatest of these
is charity.'" His love of justice is set forth with peculiar and pathetic tenderness in his reply to Douglas when they were stumping Illinois in 1858.

"Certainly," said he, "the negro is not our equal
in color; perhaps not in other respects; still, in the

right to put into his mouth the bread that his own hands have earned, he is the equal of every other man, white or black. All I ask for the negro is, that if you do not like him, let him alone. If God gave him but a little, that little let him enjoy." Can anything be more manly, honest, just, and charitable? If Lincoln read but few books, he certainly read his Bible, and kept in remembrance the Sermon on the Mount.

This gentleness and softness of heart did not make him weak. He was strong and inflexible when duty required him to be so. One of his intimate friends remarked of him that he "had the firmness, without the temper, of Jackson."

There seems to have been a strange vein of sadness underlying Mr. Lincoln's character, which affected his whole life and conduct. It was probably a constitutional dejection, rather than a grief resulting from disappointment or misfortune. This idiosyncrasy expressed itself in his homely face, for, despite the wit and humor in which he so often indulged, there was an ever-present pathos which no gayety could wholly repress. "His mirth," says his biographer, "was exuberant; it sparkled in jest, story, and anecdote, and the next moment those peculiar, sad, pathetic, melancholy eyes showed a man familiar with sorrow and acquainted with grief."

Mr. Lamon, the law-partner of Lincoln, says, "It would be difficult to recite all the causes of his melancholy disposition; that it was partly owing to physical causes there is no doubt; but his mind was filled with gloomy forebodings and strong apprehensions of impending evil, mingled with extravagant visions of personal grandeur and power. His imagination painted a scene just beyond the veil of the immediate future, gilded with glory, yet tarnished with blood. It was his destiny — splendid but dreadful, fascinating but terrible. He never doubted for a moment but he was formed for some 'great or miserable end.' He talked about it frequently, and sometimes calmly. He said the impression had grown upon him 'all his life.' The presentiment never deserted him; it was as clear, as perfect, as certain, as any image conveyed by the senses. He had entertained it so long that it was as much a part of his nature as the consciousness of identity. . . . He was to fall, and fall from a lofty place, and in the performance of a great work. The star under which he was born was at once brilliant and malignant."

The historians who shall hereafter portray the character of those who took prominent parts in our great civil war, like those who have given us the characters of the eminent men who have illustrated the annals of other nations, will paint, more or less, according to their political partialities and prejudices; but all, of whatever party or sect, who

" nothing extenuate
Nor set down aught in malice,"

must concede that Mr. Lincoln was a good and a great man; that his benevolence was large, his motives pure, his integrity unsullied, his ambition unselfish, his patriotism exalted, and that, by his prudence, sagacity, skill, and firmness, he saved the Union and preserved the republic which Washington founded.

He has gone to join the spirits of the just made perfect. He has entered the communion of the noble army of martyrs in the cause of country. He has been received into the ellowship of the illustrious of every age and nation.

No monument of granite or bronze is needed to perpetuate his memory, and hold his place in the affections of his countrymen. His fame will suffer nothing from the corrosion of time, but increase with the advancing years.

Crescit, occulto velut arbor ævo
Fama Marcelli. Micat inter omnes
Julium sidus, velut inter ignes
Luna minores.

www.ingramcontent.com/pod-product-compliance
Lightning Source LLC
Chambersburg PA
CBHW030904260626
47169CB00008B/2677